I wish
had all
born birds
instead.

-Kurt
Vonnegut

This Notebook belongs to :

Notes/Bird Photo :

Bird Photo/Sketch :

Date :

Location : --

Habitat : ---

GPS Co-ordinates : ---

Weather Conditions : ---

Birds Spotted / Quantity : ---------------------------------------

----

Birds Seen but Not Identified : -----------------------------------
(Description)

Interesting Events : --

Notes/Bird Photo :

Bird Photo/Sketch :

Date :

Location : ---

Habitat : --

GPS Co-ordinates : ---

Weather Conditions : --

Birds Spotted / Quantity : --

Birds Seen but Not Identified : ---
(Description)

Interesting Events : --

Notes/Bird Photo :

Bird Photo/Sketch :

Date :

Location : --

Habitat : --

GPS Co-ordinates : --

Weather Conditions : --

Birds Spotted / Quantity : --

Birds Seen but Not Identified : --
(Description)

Interesting Events : ---

Notes/Bird Photo :

Bird Photo/Sketch :

Date :

Location : --

Habitat : ---

GPS Co-ordinates : --

Weather Conditions : ---

Birds Spotted / Quantity : ---

Birds Seen but Not Identified : ---
(Description)

Interesting Events : ---

Notes/Bird Photo :

Bird Photo/Sketch :

Date :

Location : --

Habitat : ---

GPS Co-ordinates : --

Weather Conditions : --

Birds Spotted / Quantity : --

Birds Seen but Not Identified : --
(Description)

Interesting Events : --

Notes/Bird Photo :

Bird Photo/Sketch :

Date :

Location : --

Habitat : --

GPS Co-ordinates : ---

Weather Conditions : --

Birds Spotted / Quantity : ---

Birds Seen but Not Identified : --
(Description)

Interesting Events : ---

Notes/Bird Photo :

Bird Photo/Sketch :

Date :

Location : --

Habitat : --

GPS Co-ordinates : --

Weather Conditions : ---

Birds Spotted / Quantity : --

Birds Seen but Not Identified : --
(Description)

Interesting Events : --

Notes/Bird Photo :

Bird Photo/Sketch :

Date :

Location : --

Habitat : --

GPS Co-ordinates : --

Weather Conditions : --

Birds Spotted / Quantity : --

Birds Seen but Not Identified : --
(Description)

Interesting Events : ---

Notes/Bird Photo :

Bird Photo/Sketch :

Date :

Location :

Habitat :

GPS Co-ordinates :

Weather Conditions :

Birds Spotted / Quantity :

Birds Seen but Not Identified :
(Description)

Interesting Events :

Notes/Bird Photo :

Bird Photo/Sketch :

Date :

Location :

Habitat :

GPS Co-ordinates :

Weather Conditions :

Birds Spotted / Quantity :

Birds Seen but Not Identified :
(Description)

Interesting Events :

Notes/Bird Photo :

Bird Photo/Sketch :

Date :

Location : --

Habitat : ---

GPS Co-ordinates : ---

Weather Conditions : ---

Birds Spotted / Quantity : ---

Birds Seen but Not Identified : ---
(Description)

Interesting Events : --

Notes/Bird Photo :

Bird Photo/Sketch :

Date :

Location : --

Habitat : ---

GPS Co-ordinates : --

Weather Conditions : --

Birds Spotted / Quantity : --

Birds Seen but Not Identified : --
(Description)

Interesting Events : --

Notes/Bird Photo :

Bird Photo/Sketch :

Date :

Location : --

Habitat : ---

GPS Co-ordinates : ---

Weather Conditions : --

Birds Spotted / Quantity : ---

Birds Seen but Not Identified : --
(Description)

Interesting Events : ---

Notes/Bird Photo :

Bird Photo/Sketch :

Date :

Location : --

Habitat : ---

GPS Co-ordinates : --

Weather Conditions : ---

Birds Spotted / Quantity : --

Birds Seen but Not Identified : --
(Description)

Interesting Events : ---

Notes/Bird Photo :

Bird Photo/Sketch :

Date :

Location : ---

Habitat : --

GPS Co-ordinates : ---

Weather Conditions : --

Birds Spotted / Quantity : ---

Birds Seen but Not Identified : --
(Description)

Interesting Events : ---

Notes/Bird Photo :

Bird Photo/Sketch :

Date :

Location : --

Habitat : ---

GPS Co-ordinates : --

Weather Conditions : --

Birds Spotted / Quantity : ---

Birds Seen but Not Identified : ---
(Description)

Interesting Events : --

Notes/Bird Photo :

Bird Photo/Sketch :

Date :

Location : --

Habitat : --

GPS Co-ordinates : ---

Weather Conditions : ---

Birds Spotted / Quantity : --

Birds Seen but Not Identified : --
(Description)

Interesting Events : --

Notes/Bird Photo :

Bird Photo/Sketch :

Date :

Location : --

Habitat : --

GPS Co-ordinates : --

Weather Conditions : --

Birds Spotted / Quantity : --

Birds Seen but Not Identified : --
(Description)

Interesting Events : --

Notes/Bird Photo :

Bird Photo/Sketch :

Date :

Location : ⸻

Habitat : ⸻

GPS Co-ordinates : ⸻

Weather Conditions : ⸻

⸻

Birds Spotted / Quantity : ⸻

⸻

⸻

⸻

⸻

⸻

Birds Seen but Not Identified : ⸻
(Description)

⸻

⸻

⸻

⸻

Interesting Events : ⸻

⸻

⸻

Notes/Bird Photo :

Bird Photo/Sketch :

Date :

Location : --

Habitat : --

GPS Co-ordinates : --

Weather Conditions : ---

Birds Spotted / Quantity : ---

Birds Seen but Not Identified : ---
(Description)

Interesting Events : ---

Notes/Bird Photo :

Bird Photo/Sketch :

Date :

Location : ....

Habitat : ....

GPS Co-ordinates : ....

Weather Conditions : ....

....

Birds Spotted / Quantity : ....

....

....

....

....

Birds Seen but Not Identified : ....
(Description)

....

....

....

Interesting Events : ....

....

....

Notes/Bird Photo :

Bird Photo/Sketch :

Date :

Location : --

Habitat : --

GPS Co-ordinates : ---

Weather Conditions : --

Birds Spotted / Quantity : --

Birds Seen but Not Identified : ---
(Description)

Interesting Events : ---

Notes/Bird Photo :

Bird Photo/Sketch :

Date :

Location : --

Habitat : ---

GPS Co-ordinates : --

Weather Conditions : --

Birds Spotted / Quantity : ---

Birds Seen but Not Identified : ---
(Description)

Interesting Events : ---

Notes/Bird Photo :

Bird Photo/Sketch :

Date :

Location : --

Habitat : --

GPS Co-ordinates : ---

Weather Conditions : --

Birds Spotted / Quantity : --

Birds Seen but Not Identified : --
(Description)

Interesting Events : ---

Notes/Bird Photo :

Bird Photo/Sketch :

Date :

Location :

Habitat :

GPS Co-ordinates :

Weather Conditions :

Birds Spotted / Quantity :

Birds Seen but Not Identified :
(Description)

Interesting Events :

Notes/Bird Photo :

Bird Photo/Sketch :

Date :

Location : ⋯⋯⋯⋯⋯⋯⋯⋯⋯⋯⋯⋯⋯⋯⋯⋯⋯⋯⋯⋯⋯⋯⋯⋯⋯⋯

Habitat : ⋯⋯⋯⋯⋯⋯⋯⋯⋯⋯⋯⋯⋯⋯⋯⋯⋯⋯⋯⋯⋯⋯⋯⋯⋯⋯

GPS Co-ordinates : ⋯⋯⋯⋯⋯⋯⋯⋯⋯⋯⋯⋯⋯⋯⋯⋯⋯⋯⋯⋯⋯

Weather Conditions : ⋯⋯⋯⋯⋯⋯⋯⋯⋯⋯⋯⋯⋯⋯⋯⋯⋯⋯⋯⋯

⋯⋯⋯⋯⋯⋯⋯⋯⋯⋯⋯⋯⋯⋯⋯⋯⋯⋯⋯⋯⋯⋯⋯⋯⋯⋯⋯⋯⋯⋯⋯⋯

Birds Spotted / Quantity : ⋯⋯⋯⋯⋯⋯⋯⋯⋯⋯⋯⋯⋯⋯⋯⋯

⋯⋯⋯⋯⋯⋯⋯⋯⋯⋯⋯⋯⋯⋯⋯⋯⋯⋯⋯⋯⋯⋯⋯⋯⋯⋯⋯⋯⋯⋯⋯⋯

⋯⋯⋯⋯⋯⋯⋯⋯⋯⋯⋯⋯⋯⋯⋯⋯⋯⋯⋯⋯⋯⋯⋯⋯⋯⋯⋯⋯⋯⋯⋯⋯

⋯⋯⋯⋯⋯⋯⋯⋯⋯⋯⋯⋯⋯⋯⋯⋯⋯⋯⋯⋯⋯⋯⋯⋯⋯⋯⋯⋯⋯⋯⋯⋯

⋯⋯⋯⋯⋯⋯⋯⋯⋯⋯⋯⋯⋯⋯⋯⋯⋯⋯⋯⋯⋯⋯⋯⋯⋯⋯⋯⋯⋯⋯⋯⋯

Birds Seen but Not Identified : ⋯⋯⋯⋯⋯⋯⋯⋯⋯⋯⋯⋯
(Description)

⋯⋯⋯⋯⋯⋯⋯⋯⋯⋯⋯⋯⋯⋯⋯⋯⋯⋯⋯⋯⋯⋯⋯⋯⋯⋯⋯⋯⋯⋯⋯⋯

⋯⋯⋯⋯⋯⋯⋯⋯⋯⋯⋯⋯⋯⋯⋯⋯⋯⋯⋯⋯⋯⋯⋯⋯⋯⋯⋯⋯⋯⋯⋯⋯

⋯⋯⋯⋯⋯⋯⋯⋯⋯⋯⋯⋯⋯⋯⋯⋯⋯⋯⋯⋯⋯⋯⋯⋯⋯⋯⋯⋯⋯⋯⋯⋯

Interesting Events : ⋯⋯⋯⋯⋯⋯⋯⋯⋯⋯⋯⋯⋯⋯⋯⋯⋯⋯⋯

⋯⋯⋯⋯⋯⋯⋯⋯⋯⋯⋯⋯⋯⋯⋯⋯⋯⋯⋯⋯⋯⋯⋯⋯⋯⋯⋯⋯⋯⋯

⋯⋯⋯⋯⋯⋯⋯⋯⋯⋯⋯⋯⋯⋯⋯⋯⋯⋯⋯⋯⋯⋯⋯⋯⋯⋯⋯⋯⋯⋯

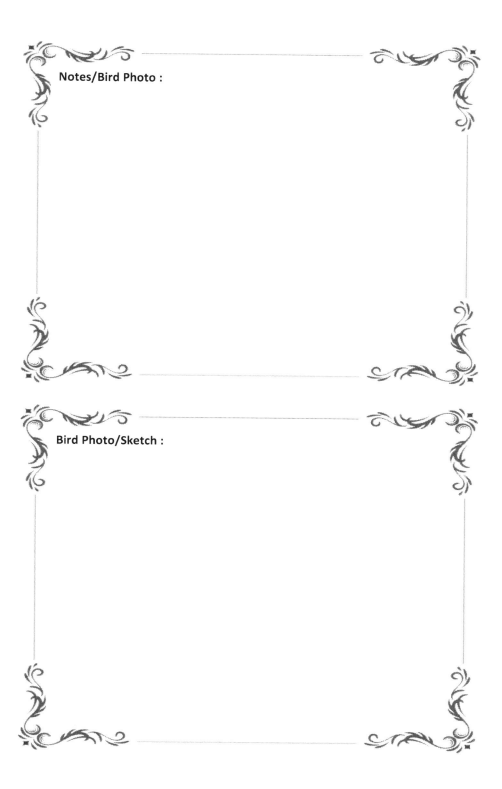

Notes/Bird Photo :

Bird Photo/Sketch :

Date :

Location : --

Habitat : --

GPS Co-ordinates : ---

Weather Conditions : --

Birds Spotted / Quantity : ---

Birds Seen but Not Identified : ---
(Description)

Interesting Events : --

Notes/Bird Photo :

Bird Photo/Sketch :

Date :

Location : ....

Habitat : ....

GPS Co-ordinates : ....

Weather Conditions : ....

....

Birds Spotted / Quantity : ....

....

....

....

....

Birds Seen but Not Identified : ....
(Description)

....

....

....

....

Interesting Events : ....

....

....

Notes/Bird Photo :

Bird Photo/Sketch :

Date :

Location : --

Habitat : --

GPS Co-ordinates : --

Weather Conditions : ---

Birds Spotted / Quantity : --

Birds Seen but Not Identified : --------------------------------------
(Description)

Interesting Events : --

Notes/Bird Photo :

Bird Photo/Sketch :

Date :

Location : --

Habitat : --

GPS Co-ordinates : ---

Weather Conditions : ---

Birds Spotted / Quantity : --

Birds Seen but Not Identified : --
(Description)

Interesting Events : ---

Notes/Bird Photo :

Bird Photo/Sketch :

Date :

Location : ---

Habitat : ---

GPS Co-ordinates : --

Weather Conditions : --

Birds Spotted / Quantity : ---

Birds Seen but Not Identified : --
(Description)

Interesting Events : ---

Notes/Bird Photo :

Bird Photo/Sketch :

Date :

Location : --

Habitat : --

GPS Co-ordinates : --

Weather Conditions : --

Birds Spotted / Quantity : ---

Birds Seen but Not Identified : ---
(Description)

Interesting Events : --

Notes/Bird Photo :

Bird Photo/Sketch :

Date :

Location : _____

Habitat : _____

GPS Co-ordinates : _____

Weather Conditions : _____

_____

Birds Spotted / Quantity : _____

_____

_____

_____

_____

Birds Seen but Not Identified : _____
(Description)

_____

_____

_____

Interesting Events : _____

_____

_____

Notes/Bird Photo :

Bird Photo/Sketch :

Date :

Location : --

Habitat : --

GPS Co-ordinates : ---

Weather Conditions : --

Birds Spotted / Quantity : --

Birds Seen but Not Identified : ---
(Description)

Interesting Events : --

Notes/Bird Photo :

Bird Photo/Sketch :

Date :

Location : --

Habitat : --

GPS Co-ordinates : ---

Weather Conditions : --

Birds Spotted / Quantity : ---

Birds Seen but Not Identified : --
(Description)

Interesting Events : ---

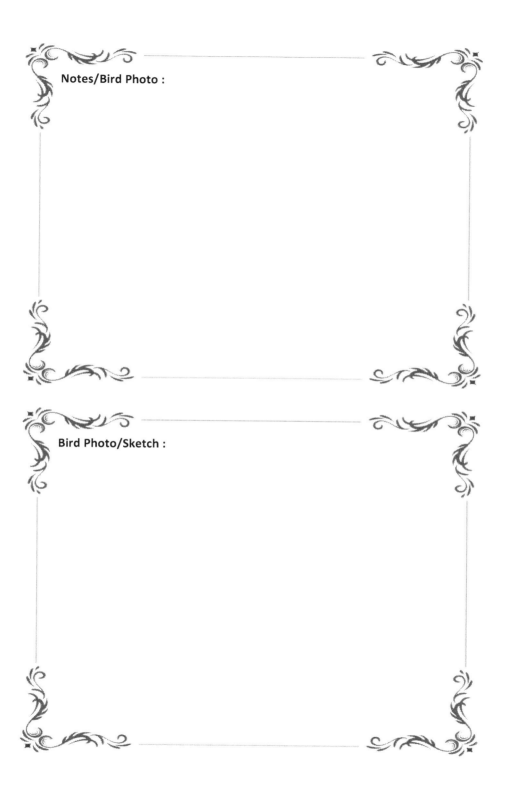

Notes/Bird Photo :

Bird Photo/Sketch :

Date :

Location : --

Habitat : --

GPS Co-ordinates : ---

Weather Conditions : --

Birds Spotted / Quantity : ---

Birds Seen but Not Identified : --------------------------------------
(Description)

Interesting Events : --

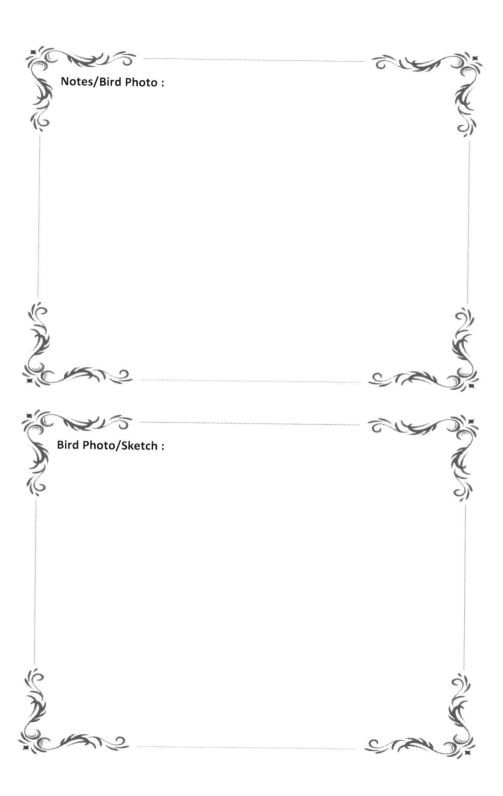

Notes/Bird Photo :

Bird Photo/Sketch :

Date :

Location :

Habitat :

GPS Co-ordinates :

Weather Conditions :

Birds Spotted / Quantity :

Birds Seen but Not Identified :
(Description)

Interesting Events :

Notes/Bird Photo :

Bird Photo/Sketch :

Date :

Location : --

Habitat : --

GPS Co-ordinates : ---

Weather Conditions : --

Birds Spotted / Quantity : ---

Birds Seen but Not Identified : ---------------------------------------
(Description)

Interesting Events : --

Notes/Bird Photo :

Bird Photo/Sketch :

Date :

Location : ---

Habitat : --

GPS Co-ordinates : --

Weather Conditions : ---

Birds Spotted / Quantity : ---

Birds Seen but Not Identified : --
(Description)

Interesting Events : ---

Notes/Bird Photo :

Bird Photo/Sketch :

Date :

Location : --

Habitat : --

GPS Co-ordinates : --

Weather Conditions : --

Birds Spotted / Quantity : --

Birds Seen but Not Identified : --
(Description)

Interesting Events : --

Notes/Bird Photo :

Bird Photo/Sketch :

Date :

Location : --

Habitat : --

GPS Co-ordinates : --

Weather Conditions : --

Birds Spotted / Quantity : --

Birds Seen but Not Identified : --
(Description)

Interesting Events : --

Notes/Bird Photo :

Bird Photo/Sketch :

Date :

Location : ---

Habitat : ---

GPS Co-ordinates : --

Weather Conditions : ---

Birds Spotted / Quantity : --

Birds Seen but Not Identified : ---
(Description)

Interesting Events : ---

Notes/Bird Photo :

Bird Photo/Sketch :

Date :

Location : ....

Habitat : ....

GPS Co-ordinates : ....

Weather Conditions : ....
....

Birds Spotted / Quantity : ....
....
....
....
....

Birds Seen but Not Identified : ....
(Description)
....
....
....

Interesting Events : ....
....
....

Notes/Bird Photo :

Bird Photo/Sketch :

Date :

Location : --

Habitat : --

GPS Co-ordinates : ---

Weather Conditions : --

Birds Spotted / Quantity : --

Birds Seen but Not Identified : --
(Description)

Interesting Events : --

Notes/Bird Photo :

Bird Photo/Sketch :

Date :

Location : ---

Habitat : --

GPS Co-ordinates : --

Weather Conditions : --

Birds Spotted / Quantity : ---

Birds Seen but Not Identified : --
(Description)

Interesting Events : ---

Notes/Bird Photo :

Bird Photo/Sketch :

Date :

Location : --

Habitat : --

GPS Co-ordinates : --

Weather Conditions : --

Birds Spotted / Quantity : --

Birds Seen but Not Identified : --------------------------------
(Description)

Interesting Events : --

Notes/Bird Photo :

Bird Photo/Sketch :

Date :

Location : --

Habitat : --

GPS Co-ordinates : --

Weather Conditions : --

Birds Spotted / Quantity : ---

Birds Seen but Not Identified : --
(Description)

Interesting Events : ---

Notes/Bird Photo :

Bird Photo/Sketch :

Date :

Location : ....

Habitat : ....

GPS Co-ordinates : ....

Weather Conditions : ....

....

Birds Spotted / Quantity : ....

....

....

....

....

Birds Seen but Not Identified : ....
(Description)

....

....

....

Interesting Events : ....

....

....

Notes/Bird Photo :

Bird Photo/Sketch :

Date :

Location : --

Habitat : --

GPS Co-ordinates : ---

Weather Conditions : --

Birds Spotted / Quantity : ---

Birds Seen but Not Identified : --
(Description)

Interesting Events : --

Printed in Poland
by Amazon Fulfillment
Poland Sp. z o.o., Wrocław